SINGLE

THE PATH TO EXCELLENCE

Author
DR. NEVILLE G. WOLLISTON

Copyright 2024 by DR. NEVILLE G. WOLLISTON and CAE Publications - All rights reserved. It is illegal to reproduce, duplicate, or transmit any part of this document in either electronic means or printed format. Recording of this publication is prohibited. Scripture reference from KJV, NIV and NLT. Dictionary references from Merriam Webster Dictionary.

CONTENTS

Introduction

1. THE VALUE OF WAITING 1
2. THE PRESENCE OF GOD 12
3. TO CLOSE TOO SOON 18
4. UNCOMPROMISING 25
5. SETTLED IN GOD 32

Introduction

According to the Bible, both singleness and marriage are callings and gifts of God. Both require individuals to have a personal relationship with God in order to fulfill their roles. Whether married or single, we are all called to have a personal relationship with God that takes priority over our relationships with others.

The gift of being single allows individuals to dedicate their lives to God and His work. The gift of marriage is designed for individuals to serve their families in a way that reflects their service to God. It is through marriage that humanity continues to come forth. God Himself is responsible for selecting our life partners, and as we align ourselves with His will, we become part of His ultimate plan, whether single or married.

Prior to God providing Adam with a wife, God and Adam shared a significant time of solitude together. It is during this time that Adam learned who he was, who God was, and what his purpose was in life. Adam's downfall resulted from his submission to a voice that was inferior to God's. He yielded to Eve's words when God had directly spoken to him. Eve's downfall, on the other hand, stemmed from her lack of a personal and intimate relationship with God. She succumbed to temptation because she did not comprehend her true worth, her purpose, and her mind lacked a firm foundation of God's teachings. Eve experienced deception due to her weakened state, which was a result of her lack of a personal relationship with God. This vulnerability stemmed from her inclination to compare herself to God and her envy towards Adam, her husband. He was fulfilling his purpose and enjoying his life, she was not.

Furthermore, her weakened state was exacerbated by her failure to acknowledge her unique role in the procreation of humanity. Deception arises when individuals fail to establish a personal relationship with God and instead rely solely on others' interpretations of Him, and what He says. To overcome this, it is important to embrace the Holy Spirit individually, God within us, and live a life with God, one of attentive listening, obedience, and diligent study of God's word. It is important to live in our God identity as individuals before embracing a collective identity(marriage). Each individual must live in oneness with God, fully aware of their God given purpose. We have been created to birth humanity and steward our responsibilities as the lineage of God.

"SINGLE: The Path to Excellence" was written to help individuals navigate the challenges and obstacles of living single in today's society. This guide offers valuable insight and strategies to help avoid the pitfalls that often hinder personal growth and fulfillment.

Chapter One

THE VALUE OF WAITING

Individuals may not realize that being single is a special gift from God. It can be challenging to be single in a world where it seems like everyone else is in a relationship. We can have confidence that our value and importance to God has nothing to do with whether or not we are married.

Our loving Father in heaven has so much more planned for our lives than just finding a partner. As individuals, we should look forward to discovering, with anticipation, the amazing life God has in store for those who trust Him.

In 1 Corinthians 7 verses 25-38, we find these words:

Now concerning virgins, I have no commandment of the Lord: yet I give my judgment, as one that hath obtained mercy of the Lord to be faithful. I suppose therefore that this is good for the present distress, I say, that it is good for a man so to be. Art, thou bound unto a wife? seek not to be loosed. Art thou loosed from a wife? seek not a wife. But and if thou marry, thou hast not sinned; and if a virgin marry, she hath not sinned. Nevertheless such shall have trouble in the flesh: but I spare you. But this I say, brethren, the time is short: it remaineth, that both they that have wives be as though they had none; And they that weep, as though they wept not; and they that rejoice, as though they rejoiced not; and they that buy, as though they possessed not; And they that use this world, as not abusing it: for the fashion of this world passeth away. But I would have you without carefulness. He that is unmarried careth for the things that belong to the Lord, how he may please the Lord: But he that is married careth for the things that are of the world, how he may please his wife. There is difference also between a wife and a virgin. The unmarried woman careth for the things of the Lord, that she may be holy both in body and in spirit: but she that is married careth for the things of the world, how she may please her husband. And this I speak for your own profit; not that I may cast a snare upon you, but for that which is comely, and that ye may attend upon the Lord without distraction. But if any man thinks that he behaveth himself uncomely toward his virgin, if she pass the flower of her age, and need so require, let him do what he will, he sinneth not: let them marry. Nevertheless, he that standeth stedfast in his heart, having no necessity, but hath power over his own will, and hath so decreed in his heart that he will keep his virgin, doeth well. So, then he that giveth her in marriage doeth well; but he that giveth her not in marriage doeth better.

According to Apostle Paul's words, it seems that he had great knowledge about being single. It makes sense since he was single himself, dedicated to God, and was the Apostle chosen by God to establish churches. In the Bible, there are many remarkable individuals, like Apostle Paul, who lived powerful, purposeful, and fulfilled lives while being single. Instead of obsessing over changing their single status to being married, singles today should focus on fulfilling their purpose and accomplishing the tasks assigned to them by God. One of the challenges faced by singles today is the difficulty in waiting. Our society is so fast-paced, where everything is instant, that we sometimes expect

God to work in the same way, leaving no room for patience. However, being single is a gift from God - a gift that should be embraced and cherished.

Many singles are waiting, but they are not waiting on God. If you are single, wait on God and not on a person. God is infallible, whereas people are not. People will fail you. If you're waiting on a person, when that person comes, he or she will surely disappoint you, it is human nature. Waiting on God is what we are required to do. During the time of waiting, we are learning who we are, who God is, what our gifts and skills are, and our purpose and value. If we rush this time of waiting, we will carry baggage, dysfunction and destruction into the marriage, home, and family, thus destroying the very union that was to be of God.

God's timing is always perfect, and He never disappoints. When single and waiting, know that God is with you and will help you to avoid temptation, but you must be willing to do your part as well. In order to be ready for the spouse God has planned for you, there are a few important things to consider. First, it is important to separate yourself from the world and follow God's excellent path for your life. Second, have patience and trust in God's perfect timing. Instead of focusing on finding a mate, prioritize your relationship with God and live out the purpose He has for you. Whether single or married, God is always there to help. Our main focus should always be on being individuals who are set apart, living a holy life that pleases God. If we desire a union established by God, we must prepare ourselves by seeking purity and aligning with God and His will. We cannot expect to receive from God that which is God's without doing what God requires.

While waiting, be attentive as well. Our time on earth is short, but our time in heaven is for eternity. How we live our lives on earth determines our eternal abode.

In verse 29, it says, *"But let me say this, my friends, time is short: it remains that both those with spouses should live as if they had none."*

Keep in mind that there are no marriages in heaven. Therefore, we must always have an eternal perspective about life. We must view life from God's eternal standpoint rather than an earthly one. Time is too short to be confined by worldly things and fleshy desires. We are spiritual beings living in an earthly body, and we must learn to live from the spiritual realm in God.

Embrace singleness; it is a gift from God. Live your best life in God at all times. Both singleness and marriage are gifts and callings from God, and both carry a high level of responsibility.

REFLECTION

Take your time to mediate on the questions below. The REFLECTION time is an opportunity to get to know yourself and understand the reasons behind your actions. The goal is not only to reflect on how you do things, but to modify your thought patterns, so that you can think in accordance with biblical principles and experience the promises God has for you. Use a journal or notebook for additional space.

How much time do you spend with God daily?

Have you accepted and embraced the gift of being single?

What are you doing to fulfill the assignments that God currently has on your life?

Knowing that your value is not predicated on being married, how are you walking in that truth? What changes do you need to make?

Chapter Two

THE PRESENCE OF GOD

Living the path to excellence requires staying in the presence of God. Failure occurs when we step out of the presence of God. God is within us, but we should also hold ourselves accountable by being with mature Christians who can hold us to God's standards. We must not neglect the opportunity to attend worship services, bible study, and prayer gatherings that are led by the Holy Spirit. This allows our faith and character to grow in God.

Many Christian singles make the mistake of not staying in the presence of God and not surrounding themselves with individuals of upright and moral character. They forfeit the guidance of accountable leaders who can hold them responsible for their journey with God.

I am reminded of the story of Adam, how God put him in a deep sleep, and when he woke up, his wife was there by his side. So, the question is, where did Eve find Adam? In the presence of God. It's important that while you are single, you remain in the presence of God. Sometimes, single Christians go looking for their partners in the wrong places: in the clubs, or bars, places that are not God-approved.

Just think about this for a moment. Wherever you find your spouse, there is a high probability that they will frequent the same places after marriage. If you found them in a club, or bar, or anywhere your Christian faith or principles might be compromised, chances are that's where they will be after marriage. But if you find them in Church, not just in the Church but in the presence of God, then you can have confidence that is the place they are likely to be during marriage.

"In the presence of the Lord, there is fullness of joy; at His right hand are pleasures forevermore."

Adam stayed in the presence of God until the woman was brought to him. Are you willing to stay in God's presence? Are you willing to make the ultimate sacrifice to receive God's best for your life? If you are willing to stay in His presence and commit yourself totally to Him, then I believe, as the Scriptures say, *"He will give you the desires of your heart."* Staying in the presence of the Lord will require not only sacrifice but also total surrender and commitment. Surrender your will, intellect, and emotions, and commit completely to His will for your life. I challenge you today to stay in the presence of the Lord as you seek and desire a mate for the next phase of your life. The Bible says, *"He will grant you the desires of your heart."* Stay in God's presence.

REFLECTION

Take your time to mediate on the questions below. The REFLECTION time is an opportunity to get to know yourself and understand the reasons behind your actions. The goal is not only to reflect on how you do things, but to modify your thought patterns, so that you can think in accordance with biblical principles and experience the promises God has for you. Use a journal or notebook for additional space.

What places have you looked for a spouse? Did you spend time in the presence of God for your spouse? If not, why not?

What changes do you need to make to live consistently in and from the presence of God?

Did God provide you with a church home? Are you actively involved in your church? Do you have a relationship with leadership? If you do not, why not? What do you need to do to be connected and stay connected?

Chapter Three

TO CLOSE TOO SOON

When dating, it is important to avoid the mistake of "getting too close too soon." There are various definitions of dating and courting, it should simply be an event between two mature individuals for observation and personal growth. There should be no expectations, escalation, or physical intimacy involved. Dating is meant for observing and learning about each other.

If you find yourself consistently seeing the same person week after week, you have transitioned from going on dates to being in a dating relationship. At this point, there may be expectations and many opportunities for temptation to arise. However, if you are not ready for the responsibilities and commitments of marriage, it's best to be cautious and not rush into a relationship. When you start dating, make sure that you are drawing closer to God more than to the other person. There is a tendency to put the relationship with God on the back burner and try to replace God with the person you're dating, but this sets you up for failure. We should never place anyone above our relationship with God. Any relationships that are not aligned in this order will fail, whether it is with family, work, friends, or anyone else.

Once you transition to dating, this means you are preparing for marriage. This is the time to discuss premarital counseling with your Church leaders. Many may say, "Well, we aren't thinking of marriage right now," but if you are not thinking of marriage, what would be the reason for dating? Dating is the prerequisite for marriage.

Unfortunately, many singles, including Christians, believe that anything is acceptable as long as both parties' consent. This leads to emotional and physical intimacy, which is not the will of God, and results in negative consequences.

Dating should be approached prayerfully, discreetly, and with supervision and accountability.

Getting too close too soon can have an adverse and unpleasant effect. While dating, one must also consider the emotional investment that is being made in the relationship. The danger with this is that usually, one would expect a withdrawal from their investment at some point. Dating should be approached prayerfully and not unadvisedly. While dating, there should also be an end goal. At what point do we cut it off, or at what point do we seek to take the relationship to the next level with wise counsel? While dating, we should always remember that we are the light and salt, and the world is watching us. We do not subscribe to the "anything goes" mentality.

When dating, it is important to ask the hard questions: Is this person God's best for my life? Did I choose this person, or did God choose them for me? Is this God's perfect OR permissive will? Most importantly, while dating, be aware and alert. Do not get too close too soon, stay close to God.

REFLECTION

Take your time to mediate on the questions below. The REFLECTION time is an opportunity to get to know yourself and understand the reasons behind your actions. The goal is not only to reflect on how you do things, but to modify your thought patterns, so that you can think in accordance with biblical principles and experience the promises God has for you. Use a journal or notebook for additional space.

As you examine your relationship with God, is there anything or any person you have placed before God? If you have, why? What do you need to do to correct it?

What was your purpose of dating in the past? Is this your current thought process? If it is, what do you need to do to change it so that you are in alignment with what God requires?

As you examine your life, are you completely obedient to God, in every area of life? If not, why? What do you need to do to ensure you are in the perfect will of God?

Why do you think it is important to be close to God when dating?

How will you determine if you are getting too close too soon? What will you do if this happens?

Chapter Four

UNCOMPROMISING

Compromise, in my opinion, is the ultimate betrayal. It betrays trust, faith, and the expectations of those who look up to you as a role model of the Christian faith, seeking guidance and direction. I am reminded of Joseph when he was tempted by the king's wife. He said, **"*How can I do such a thing and sin against my God?*"** He didn't consider the act as a sin against the king or his wife, but as a sin against God. Therefore, when it comes to compromising in matters of sex and sexuality, remember it is a sin against God.

Many Christian singles, both male and female, often find ways to justify behaviors that lead them to compromise. I have heard several statements like, "We are going to get married anyway, so what's the difference?"

– this is compromise!

In addition, it is common to hear questions like, "How do I know if we are sexually compatible?" Or "I don't know if they can have children."

-again, this is compromise!

The Bible is clear and unwavering regarding our sexual conduct. The Bible states, ***"Marriage is honorable, and the marriage bed is undefiled.'*** This reflects that marriage is a beautiful thing, and it is God's perfect plan. He created and established the laws of marriage, and no one has the authority to change that.

Compromising in the area of sex will always have a negative effect. It leaves you feeling guilty, unloved, and unclean, among other things. When we have established a solid relationship with God, just like Joseph, we will be uncompromising. Our bodies are temples where God dwells, and to sin against the body sexually is sinning against God. Yes, God forgives us, but we will still have to deal with the consequences of our sin.

To have uncompromising faith, it's important for us to study the word of God for ourselves. We must be prayerful, actively listening to God's instructions, and being quick to obey. It's also important to be accountable for our actions and choices, surrounding ourselves with leaders who will help us stay on the right path. Whether we are married or single, we must strive to have uncompromising faith, always adhering to the standards set for us.

But just as he who called you is holy, so be holy in all you do; for it is written: "Be holy, because I am holy." 1 Peter 1:15-16

You, beloved, build yourselves up in your most holy faith; pray in the Holy Spirit; keep yourselves in the love of God, waiting for the

mercy of our Lord Jesus Christ that leads to eternal life.
                    Jude 1:20-21

REFLECTION

Take your time to mediate on the questions below. The REFLECTION time is an opportunity to get to know yourself and understand the reasons behind your actions. The goal is not only to reflect on how you do things, but to modify your thought patterns, so that you can think in accordance with biblical principles and experience the promises God has for you. Use a journal or notebook for additional space.

Am I anchored enough in my relationship with God that I will not compromise on any level in life? If not, what do I need to do to ensure that I do not forfeit the destiny and promises that He has for me?

Do you think compromising on any level when dating jeopardizes the relationship in the future? Why, or why not?

Chapter Five

SETTLED IN GOD

Because many lack knowledge, they often find themselves caught up in the world's ideas about dating and marriage. However, it's important to remember that marriage is a sacred institution created by God. If God has chosen you to be married, then you must trust in Him and live your life according to His plans. On the other hand, if God has called you to be single, you must also live on the excellent path He has set before you. Our lives belong to God, and if we want the life and rewards that come with it, we must be settled in our relationship with Him, doing life according to His blueprints, not ours.

When it comes to finding a mate, many Christian singles, for a myriad reasons, decide to settle. They settle for a partner who may not be ideal, opting for less than what God has in store for them. They often say, "He or she wasn't what I had in mind, but I'll make it work." Many find themselves settling due to pressure from peers, family members, the church community, or even the ticking of their biological clock. However, we should always strive for God's best in every aspect of our lives, especially when it comes to marriage. The Bible poses the question, **"Can two walk together unless they agree?"** Settling will never bring the fulfillment or satisfaction that you truly desire. Instead, it will lead to frustration, despair, and regret. True fulfillment can only be achieved when we are firmly settled in God.

I truly believe that God wants the best for His children, especially when it comes to marriage. It's because through marriage, we create families, populate the earth, and establish the future of humanity. It's a tremendous responsibility. God has chosen us to be the ones accountable for the generations to come, therefore the future rests in our hands. We must be careful not to destroy it by neglecting God's guidance and the blueprints that He has tailored specifically for our lives. There is a specific blueprint for being single and being married. As an example, we can look to Apostle Paul, one of the greatest Apostles, who was filled with the Holy Spirit and dedicated his life to building churches for God. When it comes to marriage, we can find guidance in the word of God. One of my favorite Bible verses is found in Proverbs 3:5-6. It says, ***"Trust in the Lord with all your heart, and do not lean on your own understanding. In all your ways Him, and He will direct your paths."*** When I think of that, it gives me assurance that God has our best interests at heart. All we need to do is trust Him.

David said, ***"Some trust in chariots, some trust in horses, but we will trust in the Lord our God."*** If you truly trust the God of the universe, He will give you the desires of your heart, and you won't have time to think about settling. Settling implies that you don't trust God, His timing, or His knowledge of what is best for you. Before you take that position, remember you are talking about the God of the universe, the one who said, *"Let there be light,"* and there was light. You don't have to settle if you truly believe that the Lord will lead you in His perfect will, not His permissive will.

Whether you are single or married, it's important to have a settled relationship in God. He always wants what is best for you, and when you fully surrender and seek Him, He will guide you in the right direction. His path is truly excellent!

REFLECTION

Take your time to mediate on the questions below. The REFLECTION time is an opportunity to get to know yourself and understand the reasons behind your actions. The goal is not only to reflect on how you do things, but to modify your thought patterns, so that you can think in accordance with biblical principles and experience the promises God has for you. Use a journal or notebook for additional space, if needed.

What have you settled for in relationships in the past? Why?

What do you need to do different to ensure that you only live in the God's best for you?

What do you need to do to ensure that you walk in God's perfect path and never settle for anything less?

www.ingramcontent.com/pod-product-compliance
Lightning Source LLC
LaVergne TN
LVHW051205080426
835508LV00021B/2822